IMPACT OF THE QUR'ĀN IN MENDING
HEARTS

Shaykh Dr. Sulaymān ibn Salīmallāh ar-Ruhaylī

© Maktabatulirshad Publications, USA

All rights reserved. No part of this publication may be reproduced in any language, stored in any retrieval system or transmitted in any form or by any means, whether electronic, mechanic, photocopying, recording or otherwise, without the express permission of the copyright owner.

ISBN: 978-1-9451-7315-8

First Edition: Rajab 1437 A.H. /May 2016 C.E.

Cover Design: Pario Studios, UK

Translation by Mustafa ʿAbdul Ḥākim Lameu

Revision of Translation by ʿAbdullāh Omrān

Typesetting & formatting by Abū Sulaymān Muḥammad ʿAbdul-ʿAẓīm Ibn Joshua Baker

Printing: Ohio Printing

Subject: ʾUsūl Dīn / Qurʾān

Website: www.maktabatulirshad.com
E-mail: info@maktabatulirshad.com

Table of Contents

TRANSLITERATION TABLE 5
INTRODUCTION 8
THE GREATEST IMPACT OF THE QUR'ĀN ON HEARTS IS ACTUALIZING TAWHĪD 23
LEARNING ABOUT THE MESSENGERS OF ALLĀH 25
LEARNING ABOUT THE LIVES OF THE HAPPY AND UNHAPPY 26
LEARNING ABOUT TRUE FAITH AND RIGHTEOUS GOOD DEEDS 27
FOLLOWING WHAT ALLĀH LIKES AND AVOID WHAT ALLĀH DISLIKES 32
THE HEART CAN BE INFLICTED WITH DISEASES 37
HEEDLESSNESS AND ITS PEOPLE 46
ENGAGING HIMSELF WITH WHAT HARMS 48

THE HEARTS ARE BETWEEN TWO OF THE FINGERS OF ALLĀH 50

HIS HEART WILL BE HAPPY 52

THE MUSLIM RECITES THE QUR'ĀN A LOT 53

STARTING WITH OURSELVES 60

TRANSLITERATION TABLE

Consonants

ء	ʾ	د	d	ض	ḍ	ك	k
ب	b	ذ	dh	ط	ṭ	ل	l
ت	t	ر	r	ظ	ẓ	م	m
ث	th	ز	z	ع	ʿ	ن	n
ج	j	س	s	غ	gh	هـ	h
ح	ḥ	ش	sh	ف	f	و	w
خ	kh	ص	ṣ	ق	q	ي	y

Vowels

Short	َ	a	ِ	i	ُ	u
Long	ـَا	ā	ـِي	ī	ـُو	ū

Diphthongs	ـَو	aw	ـَي	ay

IMPACT OF THE QUR'ĀN IN MENDING HEARTS

Arabic Symbols & their meanings

حفظه الله	May Allāh preserve him
رَضِيَ اللهُ عَنْهُ	May Allāh be pleased with him (i.e. a male companion of the Prophet Muḥammad)
سُبْحَانَهُ وَتَعَالَى	Glorified & Exalted is Allāh
عَزَّ وَجَلَّ	(Allāh) the Mighty & Sublime
تَبَارَكَ وَتَعَالَى	(Allāh) the Blessed & Exalted
جَلَّ وَعَلَا	(Allāh) the Sublime & Exalted
عَلَيْهِ الصَّلَاةُ وَالسَّلَامُ	May Allāh send Blessings & Safety upon him (i.e. a Prophet or Messenger)
صَلَّى اللهُ عَلَيْهِ وَعَلَى آلِهِ وَسَلَّمَ	May Allāh send Blessings & Safety upon him and his family (i.e. Du'ā sent when mentioning the Prophet Muḥammad)

SHAYKH DR. SULAYMĀN IBN SALĪMALLĀH AR-RUHAYLĪ

رَحِمَهُ ٱللَّهُ	May Allāh have mercy upon him
رَضِيَ ٱللَّهُ عَنْهُمْ	May Allāh be pleased with them (i.e. Du'ā made for the Companions of the Prophet Muḥammad)
جَلَّ جَلَالُهُ	(Allāh) His Majesty is Exalted
رَضِيَ ٱللَّهُ عَنْهَا	May Allāh be pleased with her (i.e. a female companion of the Prophet Muḥammad)

7 | Page

بِسْمِ ٱللَّهِ ٱلرَّحْمَٰنِ ٱلرَّحِيمِ

INTRODUCTION

In the name of Allāh, the Most Gracious, the Most Merciful

Praise be to Allāh, the King, the Holy, the Source of Peace, the Most Merciful, the Most Gracious, the All-Knower, Who revealed the best of speech and made its recitation purify the heart from the filth and bad deeds. Allāh bestowed upon us the religion of Islām, perfected the religion for us and completed His favor upon us. Moreover, I testify that none has the right to be worshipped in truth, but Allāh alone, the only true Deity; and that Muḥammad is His servant and Messenger, who has been sent as a mercy to mankind. Whoever sticks to his Sunnah will be guided to the straight path. However, whoever turns away from his religion will be led astray. May Allāh send prayers and blessings are upon the Prophet (ﷺ), his family and his companions.

As for what follows:

O' righteous brothers, I would like to greet you with the greeting of Islām and the residents of Paradise, namely, *as-Salām 'alaykum wa rahmatullahi wa barakātuhu.*

O' brothers, the worthiest topic of a gathering is the one featuring the [discussion] of Allāh's statements as well as those of His Messenger. It mends hearts, sets life straight and makes one patient in the face of the bitter difficulties of life.

This meeting in this blessed Masjid is one of the righteous good deeds, which brings us closer to Allāh for the one who has good intention. We ask Allāh (سبحانه وتعالى) to grant us sincerity and make us good worshippers who listen to the speech and follow the best thereof.

O' brothers, Allāh (عز وجل) has created man to place him on earth, generations after generations, and to cultivate this earth with the *Tawhid* of Allāh

(سُبْحَانَهُوَتَعَالَىٰ). Allāh (عَزَّوَجَلَّ) created in the man a piece of flesh, if it is sound and healthy, the whole body becomes sound and healthy; but if it is corrupted, the whole body becomes corrupted, that is the heart.

This piece of flesh is very tiny but influential because the spiritual and material life of the man are based on it. This piece is susceptible to both righteousness and corruption. It may be good and sound for,

﴿ إِلَّا مَنْ أَتَى ٱللَّهَ بِقَلْبٍ سَلِيمٍ ۝ ﴾

"Who comes to Allāh with a clean heart [clean from Shirk (polytheism) and Nifāq (hypocrisy)]." [*Sūrah Ash-Shu'arā* 26:89]

Also, it may be diseased and blind,

﴿ أَفَلَمْ يَسِيرُوا۟ فِى ٱلْأَرْضِ فَتَكُونَ لَهُمْ قُلُوبٌ يَعْقِلُونَ بِهَآ أَوْ ءَاذَانٌ يَسْمَعُونَ بِهَا ۖ فَإِنَّهَا لَا تَعْمَى ٱلْأَبْصَٰرُ وَلَٰكِن تَعْمَى ٱلْقُلُوبُ ٱلَّتِى فِى ٱلصُّدُورِ ۝ ﴾

"Have they not travelled through the land, and have they hearts wherewith to understand and ears wherewith to hear? Verily, it is not the eyes that grow blind, but it is the hearts which are in the breasts that grow blind." [Sūrah Al-Hajj 22:46]

The best ones are those with good hearts that manifested itself in good appearance while the bad ones are those who manifest a good appearance, but in reality, their hearts are corrupted.

Thus, the Prophet (ﷺ) said,

إِنَّ اللهَ لَا يَنْظُرُ إِلَى أَجْسَامِكُمْ ، وَ لَا إِلَى صُوَرِكُمْ ، وَلَكِنْ يَنْظُرُ إِلَى قُلُوبِكُمْ وَ أَعْمَالِكُمْ.

"Verily, Allāh does not look at your figures, nor at your attire, but He looks at your hearts and your deeds."[1]

---

[1] Related by Muslim (2564), the Book of Virtue, Good Manners and Joining of the Ties of Relationship, the unit of prohibition of treating the Muslim unfairly and leaving him without assistance

Then the Prophet (ﷺ) pointed with his noble finger at his chest.

So, mending the appearance is based on the righteousness of hearts. If hearts are sound and healthy, the appetence becomes, therefore, sound and healthy. The Prophet (ﷺ) said,

لَا يَسْتَقِيمُ إِيمَانُ عَبْدٍ حَتَّى يَسْقِيمُ قَلْبُهُ

"Mending the faith of the servant is based on the mending of his heart."[2]

Thus, the mending of hearts is the most important thing to be considered.

The Noble Qur'ān is the best way of reforming mankind. It is the words of Allāh are sent down to the Noble Prophet, Muḥammad Ibn 'Abdullāh (ﷺ). Allāh (ﷻ) described the Noble Qur'ān

---

and despising him, and also his blood, his honor and his property. This hadith is narrated by Abū Hurayrah (رضي الله عنه).
[2] Related by Ahmad in Musnad (3/198) on the authority of Anas Ibn Mālik (رضي الله عنه). It is graded as Hassan by Shaykh Al-Albānī in As-Silsilah As-Sahīhah: (6/822).

with many characteristics referring to its greatness, graciousness and influence. Allāh (سُبْحَانَهُ وَتَعَالَى) said,

﴿ إِنَّا أَنزَلْنَٰهُ قُرْءَٰنًا عَرَبِيًّا لَّعَلَّكُمْ تَعْقِلُونَ ۝ ﴾

"Verily, We have sent it down as an Arabic Qur'ān so that you may understand." [*Sūrah Yūsuf* 12:2]

Moreover, Allāh (سُبْحَانَهُ وَتَعَالَى) says,

﴿ كِتَٰبٌ أَنزَلْنَٰهُ إِلَيْكَ مُبَٰرَكٌ لِّيَدَّبَّرُوٓا۟ ءَايَٰتِهِۦ وَلِيَتَذَكَّرَ أُو۟لُوا۟ ٱلْأَلْبَٰبِ ۝ ﴾

"(This is) a Book (the Qur'ān) which We have sent down to you, full of blessings, that they may ponder over its verses, and that men of understanding may remember." [*Sūrah Sad* 38:29]

Moreover, Allāh (سُبْحَانَهُ وَتَعَالَى) says,

IMPACT OF THE QUR'ĀN IN MENDING HEARTS

> ﴿ وَهَٰذَا كِتَٰبٌ أَنزَلْنَٰهُ مُبَارَكٌ فَٱتَّبِعُوهُ وَٱتَّقُوا۟ لَعَلَّكُمْ تُرْحَمُونَ ۝ ﴾

"And this is a blessed Book (the Qur'ān) which We have sent down, so follow it and fear Allāh (i.e. do not disobey His Orders), that you may receive mercy (i.e. be saved from the torment of Hell)." [Sūrah Al-Anām 6:155]

Allāh (عَزَّوَجَلَّ) told that the Qur'ān is blessed and ordered us to follow it. Allāh (عَزَّوَجَلَّ) clarified that His Book guides to the Straight Path, Allāh (سُبْحَانَهُ وَتَعَالَىٰ) said,

> ﴿ إِنَّ هَٰذَا ٱلْقُرْءَانَ يَهْدِى لِلَّتِى هِىَ أَقْوَمُ ﴾

"Verily, this Qur'ān guides to that which is most just and right." [Sūrah Al-Isrā' 17:9]

Look thoughtfully at the phrase **"to that which is most just and right"**, meaning the Straight Path which is denoted by Allāh's saying,

14 | Page

﴿ كِتَابٌ أُحْكِمَتْ آيَاتُهُ ﴾

"(This is) a Book, the Verses of which are perfected." [Sūrah Hud 11:1]

This Book is full of admonitions and remembrances, which have a good effect on good hearts,

﴿ لَوْ أَنزَلْنَا هَٰذَا ٱلْقُرْءَانَ عَلَىٰ جَبَلٍ لَّرَأَيْتَهُۥ خَٰشِعًا مُّتَصَدِّعًا مِّنْ خَشْيَةِ ٱللَّهِ ۚ وَتِلْكَ ٱلْأَمْثَٰلُ نَضْرِبُهَا لِلنَّاسِ لَعَلَّهُمْ يَتَفَكَّرُونَ ﴿٢١﴾ ﴾

"Had We sent down this Qurʾān on a mountain, you would surely have seen it humbling itself and rent asunder by the fear of Allāh. Such are the parables which We put forward to mankind that they may reflect." [Sūrah Al-Hashr 59:21]

Allāh's speech clarifies everything, and it is considered a healing for that which is in one's hearts,

$$ وَنَزَّلْنَا عَلَيْكَ ٱلْكِتَٰبَ تِبْيَٰنًا لِّكُلِّ شَىْءٍ وَهُدًى وَرَحْمَةً وَبُشْرَىٰ لِلْمُسْلِمِينَ ﴿٨٩﴾ $$

"And We have sent down to you the Book (the Qur'ān) as an exposition of everything, guidance, mercy, and glad tidings for those who have submitted themselves (to Allāh as Muslims)." [*Sūrah An-Naḥl* 16:89]

This book leads mankind out of darkness of disbelief into light of belief,

$$ الٓرۚ كِتَٰبٌ أَنزَلْنَٰهُ إِلَيْكَ لِتُخْرِجَ ٱلنَّاسَ مِنَ ٱلظُّلُمَٰتِ إِلَى ٱلنُّورِ بِإِذْنِ رَبِّهِمْ إِلَىٰ صِرَٰطِ ٱلْعَزِيزِ ٱلْحَمِيدِ ﴿١﴾ $$

"Alif -Lam - Ra'. (This is) a Book which We have revealed to you (O' Muḥammad (ﷺ)) in order that you might lead mankind out of darkness (of disbelief and polytheism) into light (of belief in the

Oneness of Allāh and Islamic Monotheism) by their Lord's Leave to the Path of the All-Mighty, the Owner of all Praise." [*Sūrah Ibrāhīm* 14:1]

The Noble Qur'ān contains a healing (for hearts and bodies), mending, goodness, and happiness. Without the Qur'ān, hearts cannot be reformed, Allāh (سُبْحَانَهُوَتَعَالَى) says,

﴿ وَنُنَزِّلُ مِنَ ٱلۡقُرۡءَانِ مَا هُوَ شِفَآءٌ وَرَحۡمَةٌ لِّلۡمُؤۡمِنِينَ ﴾

"And We send down of the Qur'ān that which is a healing and mercy to those who believe (in Islamic Monotheism and act on it) [*Sūrah Al-Isrā'* 17:82]

Also, Allāh (عَزَّوَجَلَّ) says,

﴿ يَٰٓأَيُّهَا ٱلنَّاسُ قَدۡ جَآءَتۡكُم مَّوۡعِظَةٌ مِّن رَّبِّكُمۡ وَشِفَآءٌ لِّمَا فِي ٱلصُّدُورِ وَهُدًى وَرَحۡمَةٌ لِّلۡمُؤۡمِنِينَ ۝ ﴾

"O' mankind! There has come to you a good advice from your Lord (i.e. the Qur'ān,

IMPACT OF THE QUR'ĀN IN MENDING HEARTS

enjoining all that is good and forbidding all that evil), and a healing for that (disease of ignorance, doubt, hypocrisy and differences) which is in your breasts, - a guidance and a mercy (explaining lawful and unlawful things) for the believers." [*Sūrah Yūnus* 10:57]

So, the Noble Qur'ān is a healing for every disease, for the hearts, and for every bad thing; it cleanses and purifies the heart.

However, there is a critical condition for the Noble Qur'ān to leave its impact on mending the heart; there must be a ready heart; Allāh (عَزَّوَجَلَّ) says,

﴿ إِنَّ فِى ذَٰلِكَ لَذِكْرَىٰ لِمَن كَانَ لَهُۥ قَلْبٌ أَوْ أَلْقَى ٱلسَّمْعَ وَهُوَ شَهِيدٌ ۝ ﴾

"Verily, therein is indeed a reminder for him who has a heart or gives ear while he is heedful." [*Sūrah Qaf* 50:37]

This stipulation must exist for the Qur'ān to have an impact on man's heart. Thus, the heart must be present all the time, and one must be heedful. Imām Al-Bukhārī has said about the Qurʾān,

لَا يَجِدُ طَعْمَهُ إِلَّا مَنْ آمَنَ بَهِ

"No one can taste the Sweetness of the Qurʾān but the one who believes in it."[3]

The Qurʾān has a great taste no one can feel but who believes in it and gives ear while he is heedful.

Ibn Al-Qayyim (رَحِمَهُ اللَّهُ) said,

إِذَا أَرَدْتَ الْإِنْتِفَاعَ بِالْقُرْآنِ: فَأَجْمِعْ قَلْبَكَ عِنْدَ تِلَاوَتِهِ وَ سِمَاعِهِ، وَ أَلْقِ سَمْعَكَ، وَاحْضُرْ حُضُورَ مَنْ يُخَاطِبُهُ مَنْ تَكَلَّمَ بِهِ سُبْحَانَهُ مِنْهُ إِلَيْهِ، فَإِنَّهُ خِطَابٌ مِنْهُ لَكَ عَلَى لِسَانِ رَسُولِهِ (صَلَّى اللهُ عَلَيْهِ وَ سَلَّمَ).

---

[3] Sahih Al-Bukhārī 9/155

"If you want to benefit from the Qurʾān, bring your whole self during reciting and hearing it, listen to it, be attentive as if Allāh speaks directly to you. It is a speech delivered by Allāh through His Messenger (ﷺ)."[4]

Allāhu Akbar! Do we feel this? Do we feel that Allāh speaks to us through this Noble Qurʾān? What a great effect it is if we believe firmly in it!

Ibn Qutaybah (رحمه الله) said,

إِذَا حَصَلَ الْمُؤَثِّرُ وَ هُوَ الْقُرْآنُ وَ الْمَحَلُّ الْقَابِلُ وَ هُوَ الْقَلْبُ الْحَيُّ وَ وُجِدَ الشَّرْطُ وَ هُوَ الْإِصْغَاءُ وَانْتَفَى الْمَانِعُ وَ هُوَ اشْتِغَالُ الْقَلْبِ وَ ذُهُولُهُ عَنْ مَعْنَى الْخَطَابِ وَ انْصِرَافُهُ عَنْهُ إِلَى شَيْءٍ آخَرَ حَصَلَ الْأَثَرُ وَ هُوَ الْإِنْتِفَاعُ وَ التَّذَكُّرُ.

---

[4] Al-Fawāʾid p. 3

"The impact of the Qur'ān, which is benefitting and remembering, is achievable should the following factors meet: the influencing factor (i.e. Qur'ān), the ready recipient (i.e. the living heart), the precondition (i.e. attentive listening), and the absence of any obstacle (i.e. the heart being occupied and distracted from the meaning of the Qur'ān to another thing."[5]

Many people say, **"We hear the Qur'ān, but it does not cause us any reverence or remembrance."** This statement indicates that they are undutiful to Allāh. The Noble Qur'ān has a great impact on the heart if all the factors mentioned above are met.

Many people recite the Qur'ān while they are absent minded; the tongue may utter the words of the Qur'ān, but the heart is absent. So, how is it possible for such heart to receive the effect of the Qur'ān?!

---

[5] Al-Fawā'id p. 3

Thus, we should mend our hearts during the recitation of the Qur'ān through making our hearts ready for accepting the words of Allāh (سُبْحَانَهُوَتَعَالَىٰ), our ears attentive and our hearts alive, and to try hard to forget about distractions the Shayṭān is so eager to engulf us with.

Usually, when the Muslim wants to recite the Qur'ān, Shayṭān comes whispering, "Remember so and so, do so and so, think in so and so, the Ummah suffers from so and so, the people need so and so," why? He wants to keep him away from hearing the words of Allāh and reflecting upon it. Satan knows well that if the Muslim listened to the words of Allāh, it would make deviating him very difficult and the [chances of] driving him to disobey Allāh would be close to impossible.

Hearts can be mended by two ways: purification through ridding of bad traits and habits and beautification through acquiring new good ones.

SHAYKH DR. SULAYMĀN IBN SALĪMALLĀH AR-RUHAYLĪ

THE GREATEST IMPACT OF THE QUR'ĀN ON HEARTS IS ACTUALIZING TAWHĪD

The greatest impact of the Qurʾān on hearts lies in actualizing Tawhīd and freeing oneself from Shirk (polytheism) and polytheists.

The science of Tawhīd, including the grandeur traits of Allāh, are considered the greatest Qurʾānic science. When one reflects upon Ayāt of Tawhid and the Names and Attributes of Allāh and reflects upon the meanings of these Ayāt, this will have a great effect on his heart, and will cause him do righteous good deeds.

When one tries strenuously to understand these Ayāt and their meanings and affirms the attributes of Allāh in a way that suits His Grandeur, his heart will be full of belief in Allāh (سُبْحَانَهُوَتَعَالَى) and love for Him. Also, one will be certain that there is none has the right to be worshipped but Allāh. Eventually, one's heart will be full of righteousness, goodness and assurance. In short, one's heart cannot be set right without believing in the Oneness of Allāh, the Lord of the worlds.

The more genuine one's Tawhīd of Allāh with a sound creed, the more his heart will be set right. Significantly, the heart is created to recognize, love, believe in the Oneness of his Creator, and so that Allāh would become its most beloved and the One to whom one resorts to. Once all of those are achieved, the heart will enjoy happiness, goodness, and tranquility.

SHAYKH DR. SULAYMĀN IBN SALĪMALLĀH AR-RUHAYLĪ

LEARNING ABOUT THE MESSENGERS OF ALLĀH

Furthermore, the impact of the Qurʾān is even greater when one learns about the Messengers of Allāh (عَلَيْهِمُٱلسَّلَامُ), how they behaved, their encounters with their friends and enemies, their characteristics and upright morals. Such knowledge will induce its carrier to love the Messengers of Allāh and follow their example. Eventually, the heart who loves them will have as much goodness as his degree of love and adherence to the path of the Messengers. The greatest one of them is Muḥammad Ibn ʿAbdullāh (صَلَّىٱللَّهُعَلَيْهِوَسَلَّمَ), if one learns about his life, manners, and actions, love and adherence will be the result of such knowledge.

LEARNING ABOUT THE LIVES OF THE HAPPY AND UNHAPPY

Moreover, the impact of the Qur'ān increases when one learns about the lives of those who are happy and those who are unhappy in this life and the life to come, learning about their lifestyles and how they got rejoiced in this life, and the high rank they obtained in the hereafter. This influences the heart to follow their example.

Along the same lines, one should learn about the lives of the bad people and how they became in this bad state. This will result in disliking them, their ways and abandon their characteristics. This is an easy way to enter paradise and to be saved from hellfire. This is one of the greatest effects of the Qur'ān on the hearts of the servants.

LEARNING ABOUT TRUE FAITH AND RIGHTEOUS GOOD DEEDS

Throughout the Qurʾān, one can learn that the only recognizable measures [of happiness] are true faith and righteous good deeds. It is not by mere claims [of faith], nor by following the ways of the Satan. Qurʾān teaches the servant that it is all about one's righteous lifestyle and sound faith. However, judging by empty claims and falling for the illusion of plentiful worldly earnings granted by Allāh to His servant is the way of the unguided people, which cannot result in goodness.

If you want to know who you really are, consider the reality of belief in your heart, and how you regard righteous good deeds.

The Qurʾān made it clear for us. Allāh says,

$$\text{﴿ وَمَا أَمْوَالُكُمْ وَلَا أَوْلَادُكُم بِالَّتِي تُقَرِّبُكُمْ عِندَنَا زُلْفَىٰ إِلَّا مَنْ ءَامَنَ وَعَمِلَ صَالِحًا فَأُولَٰئِكَ لَهُمْ جَزَاءُ الضِّعْفِ بِمَا عَمِلُوا وَهُمْ فِي الْغُرُفَاتِ ءَامِنُونَ ۝ ﴾}$$

"And it is not your wealth, nor your children that bring you nearer to Us (i.e. please Allāh), but who believes (in the Islāmic Monotheism), and does righteous deeds (will please Us); as for such, there will be twofold reward for what they did, and they will reside in the high dwellings (Paradise) in peace and security." [Sūrah Saba' 34:37]

Your lineage will not bring you nearer to Allāh,

$$\text{وَ مَنْ بَطَّأَ بِهِ عَمَلُهُ ، لَمْ يُسَرِّعْ بِهِ نَسَبُهُ}$$

"And he who lags behind in doing good deeds, his noble lineage will not make him go ahead."[6]

It is not the high position or the wealth that brings you closer to Allāh. It is rather the true belief in Allāh and the righteous good deeds. The unhappy ones are those who relied on the false claims. Allāh (عَزَّوَجَلَّ) said about the Christians and the Jews,

$$\text{﴿ وَقَالُوا۟ لَن يَدْخُلَ ٱلْجَنَّةَ إِلَّا مَن كَانَ هُودًا أَوْ نَصَرَىٰ ۗ تِلْكَ أَمَانِيُّهُمْ ۗ قُلْ هَاتُوا۟ بُرْهَـٰنَكُمْ إِن كُنتُمْ صَـٰدِقِينَ ﴾ ﴿١١١﴾}$$

"And they say, "None shall enter Paradise unless he is a Jew or a Christian." These are their own desires. Say (O Muḥammad

---

[6] Related by Muslim (2699) in the book pertaining to Remembrance of Allāh and Supplication, chapter of the grace of gathering to recite the Noble Qur'ān and Remembrance of Allah. Narrated by Abī Hurayrah (رَضِيَ ٱللَّهُ عَنْهُ).

(ﷺ)), "Produce your proof if you are truthful." [Sūrah Al-Baqarah 2:111]

No one will enter Paradise unless he produces his proof, which is a sound belief and righteous good deeds,

﴿بَلَىٰ مَنْ أَسْلَمَ وَجْهَهُ لِلَّهِ وَهُوَ مُحْسِنٌ فَلَهُ أَجْرُهُ عِندَ رَبِّهِ وَلَا خَوْفٌ عَلَيْهِمْ وَلَا هُمْ يَحْزَنُونَ ۝﴾

"Yes, but whoever submits his face (himself) to Allāh (i.e. follows Allāh's Religion of Islamic Monotheism) and he is Muḥsin then his reward is with his Lord (Allāh), on such shall be no fear, nor shall they grieve." [Sūrah Al-Baqarah 2:112]

Allāh (عَزَّوَجَلَّ) says,

﴿لَّيْسَ بِأَمَانِيِّكُمْ وَلَا أَمَانِيِّ أَهْلِ ٱلْكِتَٰبِ مَن يَعْمَلْ سُوءًا يُجْزَ بِهِ﴾

> "It will not be in accordance with your desires (Muslims), nor those of the people of the Scripture (Jews and Christians), whosoever works evil, will have the recompense thereof," [*Sūrah An-Nisā' 4:123*]

This means that being misled by [empty] claims and [face] appearances are a cause of deviation, and it is the way of deviants.

True faith and righteous good deeds are what brings a person closer to Allāh. Knowledge of such matter is a strong motivator for the heart to earnestly contemplating the Qur'ān. In the end, the heart will be pure, adherent to good deeds, and distant from all sorts of evil.

FOLLOWING WHAT ALLĀH LIKES AND AVOID WHAT ALLĀH DISLIKES

Qur'ān teaches the individual to follow what Allāh likes and avoid what Allāh dislikes. By achieving this factor, Allāh will set his heart right, and grant him what is better.

So, through the recitation of the Qur'ān, one will know that Allāh will recompense the individual who abandoned something voluntarily for His sake better than what he left. This will affect the mending of the heart. In other words, one will prefer what Allāh likes to what he likes while fully knowing that is better for him in this life and the one to come.

Consider carefully what Allāh mentioned about the Muhajirun (those who migrated from Makkah to Al-Madīnah) who left their country, property and friends for the sake of Allāh (سُبْحَانَهُ وَتَعَالَى). They loved their country where they lived. They loved their families and their possessions, but they left and emigrated for the sake of Allāh. Therefore, Allāh granted them soul tranquility and firm belief.

One of the kings offered one of the Muhajirun captivated by him a bribe,

- أَ تَتْرُكُ دِينَ مُحَمَّدٍ وَ أُعْطِيكَ نِصْفَ مُلْكِي ؟
وَ قَدْ كَانَ وَقَعَ أَسِيراً عِنْدَ ذَلِكَ الْمَلَكِ - أَ تَتْرُكُ دِينَ مُحَمَّدٍ وَ أُعْطِيكَ نِصْفَ مُلْكِي ؟ فَقَالَ : اِخْسَأْ عَدُوَّ اللهِ ، فَوَ الَّذِي نَفْسِي بِيَدِهِ لَوْ أَعْطَيْتَنِي مُلْكَكَ وَ مُلْكَ الْعَرَبِ وَ مُلْكَ الْعَجَبِ وَ مَا فِي الْأَرْضِ جَمِيعِهَا مَا تَرَكْتُ دِينَ مُحَمَّدٍ طَرْفَةَ عَيْنٍ .

"Once you abandon the religion of Muḥammad (ﷺ), I will give you half of my kingdom." He replied, "Shut up, enemy of Allāh, even if you gave me half of your kingdom and that of the Arabs and the Non-Arabs and all that on earth, I would

never leave the religion of Muḥammad (ﷺ)."[7]

This righteousness in the heart yielded the kind of certainty that whoever prefers what Allāh likes to what he likes, Allāh will grant him better things. He will be given peacefulness in heart, firm belief, and plentiful means and welfare.

- For example, when 'Ibrāhīm (عَلَيْهِ ٱلسَّلَامُ) abandoned his people and his father and what they worshipped along with Allāh, Allāh blessed him to have 'Isḥāq, Ya'qūb and the righteous offspring.

- When Yūsuf kept himself away from having this evil act with the wife of Al-Aziz, who sought to seduce him, closed the doors and said to him "Come on, O you." Also, she was

---

[7] This great companion is called 'Abdullāh Ibn Huzafa. This story is related by Ibn 'Asaakir in his history by way of Bayhaqī and Al-Hafiz in "Al-Issaba." There is also a supporting hadith of Ibn Abbas related by Ibn 'Asaakir and Ibn Al-Atheer in "Ussd Al-Ghaba" 3/212.

seducing him by her beauty and power. She promised to give him power, though he turned her down and preferred to be imprisoned. In return, Allāh gave him full authority in the land, to take possession therein, and enjoy whatever Allāh made lawful.

- Another example, when the people of the Cave abandoned disbelievers and that which they worshipped besides Allāh, Allāh opened a way for them from His Mercy, and smoothed their affair, and made them a mean for guiding the misguided. So, all the good deeds of those whom they guided are put in their scales.

- When Maryam Bint Imran guarded her chastity, Allāh breathed into (the sleeves of) her (shirt or garment) [through Jibril], and He made her and her son [Isa] a sign for Al-Alamin (the mankind and jinn).

- When the horses distracted Sulaymān from remembering Allāh (in Asr prayer). He slaughtered them because of this distraction. In return, Allāh subjected to him the wind, which blew by his order in addition to the devils from the jinn, (including) every kind of builder and diver.

So, whoever abandons his desire for the sake of Allāh (سُبْحَانَهُوَتَعَالَ), Allāh will grant him a love for Him and worship and good living in this world. If one knows this through the recitation of the Qur'ān, this will affect a huge impact of righteousness in his heart.

THE HEART CAN BE INFLICTED WITH DISEASES

Also, through the recitation of the Qur'ān, one will come to learn that the heart can be inflicted with diseases. One will, therefore, be careful to watch carefully for the [spiritual] health of his heart and try to avoid all bad traits and diseases of the heart.

Disease is divided into two types:

- Disease of doubts
- Disease of desires

Doubts: One's heart is inflicted with these doubts that keep the heart away from Allāh.

Desires: Weakness of the heart in the face of worldly interests, which causes him to commit sins.

Unfortunately, one's heart may be inflicted with both of them. However, the disease of doubt is much more dangerous because it may lead to the Shirk, the worst injustice. It also causes one to turn away from the Prophetic Sunnah. It may lead to innovation, which darkens the heart. For this reason, the Salaf said,

مَنْ جَلَسَ إِلَى صَاحِبٍ بِدْعَةٍ، أَوْرَثَهُ اللهُ الْعَمَى

"Whoever sits with an innovator, Allāh will inflict him with blindness of heart."[8]

The innovator only leads astray and evil deeds, which causes the blindness of heart.

Thus, the salaf warned against innovations and innovators and advised not to sit with innovators.

If innovations are rooted in the heart, they darken the heart so much that one would make irrational statements. Some of the innovators once said, "The Wali (righteous individual) can create a baby in a mother's womb!" Can you believe this?! The pre-Islāmic people had not even made such statements, but they said, "Allāh (سُبْحَانَهُ وَتَعَالَى) is the only Creator."

The fact is that innovation makes one's heart and mind dark. It leads the innovator say and does

---

[8] Al-Ibanah 2/460. It is narrated by Al-Fuḍayl Ibn 'Iyāḍh.

things rejected by rational thinking let alone Sharia rulings.

As for the disease of desires, it may seem insignificant, but, in fact, it creeps into the heart and darkens it unless one repents. The Prophet (ﷺ) said,

إِنَّ الْعَبْدَ إِذَا أَخْطَأَ خَطِيئَةً نُكِتَتْ فِي قَلْبِهِ نُكْتَةٌ سَوْدَاءُ، فَإِذَا هُوَ نَزَعَ وَ اسْتَغْفَرَ وَ تَابَ صُقِلَ قَلْبُهُ، وَ إِنْ عَادَ زِيدَ فِيهَا حَتَّى تَعْلُوَ قَلْبَهُ.

"Verily, when the servant commits a sin, a black spot appears on his heart. When he refrains from it, seeks forgiveness and repents, his heart is polished clean. However, if he returns, it increases until it covers his entire heart."[9]

---

[9] Related by At-Tirmidhī in Sunan (3334), the Book pertaining the Tafsīr of the Quran, the chapter pertaining part of the Sūrah

So, do not misunderstand what is said by the scholars that, **"The disease of doubts is more severe than the disease of desires,"** because they did not mean to belittle of the disease of desires. They rather meant that the disease of doubts is much more dangerous. Moreover, the disease of desires has a fatal impact on the heart. One should not be deceived by the minor sins because it leads to more major ones. The Prophet (ﷺ) said,

لَعَنَ اللهُ السَّارِقَ، يَسْرِقُ الْبَيْضَةَ فَتُقْطَعُ يَدُهُ، وَيَسْرِقُ الْحَبْلَ فَتُقْطَعُ يَدُهُ.

"May Allāh curse the thief who steals an egg for which his hands is cut off, or steals a rope for which his hands is to be cut off."[10]

---

of Wayl Lil Mutaffifin. Narrated by Abū Hurayrah. At-Tirmidhī said, "This Ḥadīth is Hassan and Ṣaḥīḥ."

[10] Agreed upon. Related by Al-Bukhārī (6401) in the Book pertaining Hudūd (punishments set by Allah), the chapter pertaining: the thief is cursed if he is anonymous. Related by Muslim (1687), the Book pertaining Hudūd, the chapter

It is clear that the egg and the rope do not reach the amount which causes cutting off the hands. The reason is that who steals an egg may steal what is bigger till [he reaches the limit required for] the hands to be cut off.

So, be careful of the minor sins, because they may lead to the major ones, which causes the blindness of the heart.

خَلِّ الذُّنُوبَ صَغِيرَهَا   وَ كَبِيرَهَا ، فَهُوَ التُّقَى

وَاصْنَعْ كَمَاشٍ فَوْقَ أَرْضٍ   الشَّوْكِ يَحْذَرُ مَا يَرَى

لَا تَحْقِرَنَّ صَغِيرَةً   إِنَّ الْجِبَالَ مِنَ الْحَصَى

Abandon all the sins,

minor or major, for it is piety.

And behave as if one walks on the earth,

---

pertaining the punishment of theft and its quota. Narrated by Abu Huraira.

where there is a thistle, he will be careful of it.

Do not belittle any sin,

Many little stones make up mountains.[11]

Another poet said[12],

رَأَيْتُ الذُّنُوبَ تُمِيتُ الْقُلُوب ** وَ قَدْ يُورِثُ الذُّلَّ إِدْمَانُهَا

وَ تَرْكُ الذُّنُوبِ حَيَاةُ الْقُلُوبِ ** وَ خَيْرٌ لِنَفْسِكَ عِصْيَانُهَا

"sins cause the spiritual death of the heart,

Humiliation is the inevitable result of its addiction.

Abandoning sins brings life to the heart.

Better for yourself to disobey your Self."

---

[11] These lines are mentioned in the Book of (Tabsirah) by Ibn El-Jawzi, p. 241.
[12] These lines are mentioned in (Al-Jawab Al-Kāfī) by Ibn Al-Qayyim p. 30

Allāh (عَزَّوَجَلَّ) mentioned in the Qurʾān the diseases that may inflict the heart. Also, Allāh clarified that the hearts are inflicted with disease of doubts, Allāh (عَزَّوَجَلَّ) says,

$$\text{﴿ فِى قُلُوبِهِم مَّرَضٌ فَزَادَهُمُ ٱللَّهُ مَرَضًا ﴾}$$

"In their hearts is a disease (of doubt and hypocrisy) and Allāh has increased their disease." [Sūrah Al-Baqarah 2:10]

Allāh (سُبْحَانَهُ وَتَعَالَى) says,

$$\text{﴿ وَأَمَّا ٱلَّذِينَ فِى قُلُوبِهِم مَّرَضٌ فَزَادَتْهُمْ رِجْسًا إِلَىٰ رِجْسِهِمْ وَمَاتُوا۟ وَهُمْ كَٰفِرُونَ ۝ ﴾}$$

"But as for those in whose hearts is a disease (of doubt, disbelief, and hypocrisy), it will add suspicion and doubt to their suspicion, belief, and doubt; and they die while they are disbelievers." [Sūrah At-Tawbah 9: 125]

Also, hearts can be inflicted with the disease of desires. Allāh (سُبْحَانَهُ وَتَعَالَى) says,

﴿ فَلَا تَخْضَعْنَ بِالْقَوْلِ فَيَطْمَعَ ٱلَّذِى فِى قَلْبِهِۦ مَرَضٌ وَقُلْنَ قَوْلًا مَّعْرُوفًا ﴾ ﴿٣٢﴾

"Then be not soft in speech, lest he in whose heart is a disease (of hypocrisy, or evil desire for adultery) should be moved with desire, but speak in an honorable manner." [Sūrah Al-Ahzāb 33:32]

So, the heart can be inflicted with the disease of doubt and the disease of evil desire, which can be cured by the Qur'ān, Allāh's words.

Ibn Al-Qayyim (رَحِمَهُ ٱللَّهُ) said,

جِمَاعُ أَمْرَاضِ الْقُلُوبِ : هُوَ أَمْرَاضُ الشُّبَهَاتِ وَالشَّهَوَاتِ ، وَ الْقُرْآنُ شِفَاءٌ لِلنَّوْعَيْنِ ، فِيهِ مِنَ الْبَيِّنَاتِ وَ الْبَرَاهِينَ الْقَطْعِيَّةِ مَا يُبَيِّنُ الْحَقَّ مِنَ الْبَاطِلِ ، فَتَزُولُ أَمْرَاضُ الشُّبْهَةِ ، وَ أَمَّا

شِفَاؤُهُ لِمَرْضِ الشَّهَوَاتِ فَذَلِكَ بِمَا فِيهِ مِنَ الْحِكْمَةِ وَ الْمَوْعِظَةِ الْحَسَنَةِ وَ التَّزْهِيدِ فِي الدُّنْيَا وَ التَّرْغِيبِ فِي الْآخِرَةِ.

"All diseases of the heart are divided into two types: (1) diseases of doubt and (2) evil desires. All of them can be cured by the Qur'ān, in which clear evidence distinguish the truth from the falsehood. So, the diseases of doubts will be cured. The Qur'ān also cures the disease of evil desire, because it contains wisdom, fair preaching, call to turn away from this world and doing righteous deeds for the hereafter"."[13]

---

[13] Ighathat Al-Lahfan, p.40.

HEEDLESSNESS AND ITS PEOPLE

Moreover, Allāh (عَزَّوَجَلَّ) warned us of heedlessness and the heedless people in the Qur'ān. Allāh says,

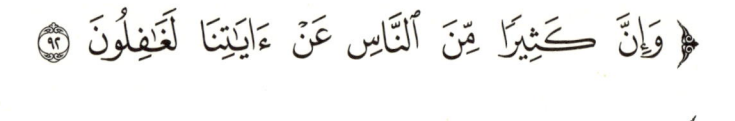

﴿ وَإِنَّ كَثِيرًا مِّنَ ٱلنَّاسِ عَنْ ءَايَٰتِنَا لَغَٰفِلُونَ ۝ ﴾

"And verily, many among mankind are heedless of Our Ayat (proofs, evidences, verses, lessons, signs, revelations, etc.)."
[Sūrah Yunus 10:92]

Allāh says,

﴿ وَلَا تَكُن مِّنَ ٱلْغَٰفِلِينَ ۝ ﴾

"And be not of those who are neglectful."
[Sūrah Al-Anfal 8:205]

Allāh says,

﴿ وَلَا تُطِعْ مَنْ أَغْفَلْنَا قَلْبَهُۥ عَن ذِكْرِنَا وَٱتَّبَعَ هَوَىٰهُ وَكَانَ أَمْرُهُۥ فُرُطًا ۝ ﴾

"And obey not him whose heart We have made heedless of Our remembrance, and who follows his own lusts, and whose affair (deeds) has been lost." [*Sūrah Al-Kahf* 18:28]

ENGAGING HIMSELF WITH WHAT HARMS

The Qurʾān teaches the individual that he will be afflicted to engage himself in what harms him, far away from what benefits him if he abandons what benefits him and doing good deeds. It also teaches that whoever misplaces the blessings of Allāh with sinning, these blessings will turn to be cursed.

Allāh (عَزَّوَجَلَّ) clarified that when the disbelievers turned away from worshipping Allāh, they worshipped the idols. Moreover, when the disbelievers were offered the opportunity to of faith at the beginning, they rejected it. Their punishment is that Allāh turned their hearts away from guidance and sealed them up so that they will not believe until they see the painful torment.

Moreover, when the Straight Path were clarified for them, they willingly kept away from it. Therefore, they were punished by the deviation of their hearts and uncertainty.

Also, when they disrespected the Ayat and Messengers of Allāh, Allāh punished them with a humiliating punishment. When they did not follow the truth, Allāh humiliated them in this life and the life to come. And when they forbade remembering and glorifying Allāh's Name in His place of worship, it was befitting they enter them with fear engulfing their hearts.

So, the legal rule that the Qur'ān lays down is that whoever is enabled to do righteous good deeds but refrains from doing so, Allāh (عَزَّوَجَلَّ) will inflict him with evils and deprive him of goodness.

IMPACT OF THE QUR'ĀN IN MENDING HEARTS

THE HEARTS ARE BETWEEN TWO OF THE FINGERS OF ALLĀH

Hearts can be reformed by the Qur'ān when one knows that the hearts are between two of the fingers of Allāh; He changes them as He wills. So, one will beseech Allāh to grant him guidance,

﴿رَبَّنَا لَا تُزِغْ قُلُوبَنَا بَعْدَ إِذْ هَدَيْتَنَا وَهَبْ لَنَا مِن لَّدُنكَ رَحْمَةً إِنَّكَ أَنتَ ٱلْوَهَّابُ ۝﴾

"Our Lord! Let not our hearts deviate (from the truth) after You have guided us, and grant us mercy from You. Truly, You are the Bestower." [*Sūrah Al-'Imrān* 3:8]

Also, the Prophet (ﷺ) used to say this supplication a lot,

يَا مُقَلِّبَ الْقُلُوبِ ثَبِّتْ قَلْبِي عَلَى دِينِكَ

"O Changer of the Hearts! Strengthen my heart upon Your Religion".[14]

---

[14] Related by At-Tirmidhī (3522), the Book pertaining supplications, the chapter pertaining Abū Mūsā al-Ansārī told us, it is graded as Ṣaḥīḥ by At-Tirmidhī and also Ad-Dhahabī. It is graded as Sahih by Al-Albani in Ṣaḥīḥ Al-Jami' (6/309) and Ṣaḥīḥ At-Tirmidhī (3/171).

HIS HEART WILL BE HAPPY

Furthermore, the heart can be mended by the Qurʾān if one knows that his heart will be happy when he wishes goodness for all Muslims and empties it from all bad manners. Allāh (عَزَّوَجَلَّ) says,

﴿ وَٱلَّذِينَ جَآءُو مِنۢ بَعْدِهِمْ يَقُولُونَ رَبَّنَا ٱغْفِرْ لَنَا وَلِإِخْوَٰنِنَا ٱلَّذِينَ سَبَقُونَا بِٱلْإِيمَٰنِ وَلَا تَجْعَلْ فِى قُلُوبِنَا غِلًّا لِّلَّذِينَ ءَامَنُوا۟ رَبَّنَآ إِنَّكَ رَءُوفٌ رَّحِيمٌ ﴾

"And those who came after them say, "Our Lord! Forgive us and our brethren who have preceded us in Faith, and put not in our hearts any hatred against those who have believed. Our Lord! You are indeed full of kindness, Most Merciful." [*Sūrah Al-Hashr* 59:10]

SHAYKH DR. SULAYMĀN IBN SALĪMALLĀH AR-RUHAYLĪ

THE MUSLIM RECITES THE QUR'ĀN A LOT

Also, hearts can be reformed by the Qur'ān when the Muslim recites the Qur'ān a lot and befriends it so much that it would consume most of his time. Such will keep his heart calm and tranquil. Allāh says,

﴿ ٱلَّذِينَ ءَامَنُواْ وَتَطْمَئِنُّ قُلُوبُهُم بِذِكْرِ ٱللَّهِ أَلَا بِذِكْرِ ٱللَّهِ تَطْمَئِنُّ ٱلْقُلُوبُ ۝ ﴾

"Those who believed (in the Oneness of Allāh – Islamic Monotheism), and whose hearts find rest in the remembrance of Allāh: verily, in the remembrance of Allāh do hearts find rest." [Sūrah Ar-Ra'd 13:28]

The Prophet (ﷺ) said,

وَ مَا اجْتَمَعَ قَوْمٌ فِي بَيْتٍ مِنْ بُيُوتِ اللهِ، يَتْلُونَ كِتَابَ اللهِ، وَ يَتَدَارَسُونَهُ بَيْنَهُمْ، إِلَّا نَزَلَتْ عَلَيْهِمُ السَّكِينَةُ، وَ غَشِيَتْهُمُ الرَّحْمَةُ وَ حَفَّتْهُمُ الْمَلَائِكَةُ، وَ ذَكَرَهُمُ اللهُ فِيمَنْ عِنْدَهُ.

"Any group of people that assemble in one of the Houses of Allāh to recite the Book of Allāh, learning and teaching it, tranquility, will descend upon them, mercy will engulf them; angels will surround them, and Allāh will make mention of them to those (the angels) in His proximity."[15]

Tranquility is something Allāh descends upon one's heart; that makes it calm and free from worries. It also makes one happy and firmly believes in Allāh. Allāh said,

---

[15] Related by Muslim (4873), the Book pertaining to the Remembrance of Allāh, Supplication, Repentance and Seeking Forgiveness, the chapter pertaining to assembling for reciting the Qur'ān. Narrated by Abū Hurayrah (ﷺ).

﴿ هُوَ ٱلَّذِىٓ أَنزَلَ ٱلسَّكِينَةَ فِى قُلُوبِ ٱلْمُؤْمِنِينَ لِيَزْدَادُوٓا۟ إِيمَـٰنًا مَّعَ إِيمَـٰنِهِمْ ﴾

"It is He Who sent down As-Sakīnah (calmness and tranquillity) into the hearts of the believers, that they may grow more in Faith along with their (present) Faith." [*Sūrah Al-Fatḥ* 48:4]

So, the remembrance of Allāh, particularly reciting the Qurʾān, descends calmness and mercy on the heart. These two elements have a great impact on the heart.

So, we should recite the Qurʾān a lot, and choose the best time for reciting it. We should not dedicate the shortest time for the recitation of the Qurʾān. We should contemplate the Words of Allāh.

Thus, goodness, happiness and benefit in this life and the one to come can be obtained through reciting the Qurʾān. Our hearts can find nothing as fruitful for its benefit other than the speech of Allāh.

Imām Ibn Al-Qayyim (رَحِمَهُ اللَّهُ) said,

لَا شَيْءَ أَنْفَعُ لِلْقَلْبِ مِنْ قِرَاءَةِ الْقُرْآنِ بِالتَّدَبّرِ وَ التَّفَكَّرِ، فَإِنَّهُ يُورِثُ الْمَحَبَّةَ وَ الشَّوْقَ وَ الْخَوْفَ وَ الرَّجَاءَ وَ الْإِنَابَةَ وَ التَّوَكَّلَ وَ الرِّضَا وَ التَّفْوِيضَ وَ الشُّكْرَ وَ الصَّبْرَ وَ سَائِرَ الْأَحْوَالِ الَّتِي بِهَا حَيَاةُ الْقَلْبِ وَ كَمَالُهُ.

"Nothing can be beneficial to the heart like reciting the Qurʾān meditatively. It causes one to have love for Allāh, passion, fear, beseeching Allāh, reliance upon Him, satisfaction, gratefulness to Allāh and patience, in addition to all everything that puts life into the heart."[16]

Qurʾān also keeps heart away from bad manners and sins that cause the spiritual death of the heart. Ibn Al-Qayyim (رَحِمَهُ اللَّهُ) said,

---

[16] Miftāh Dār as-Sʿādah p. 187.

فَلَوْ عَلِمَ النَّاسُ مَا فِي قِرَاءَةِ الْقُرْآنِ بِالتَّدَبُّرِ لَاشْتَغَلُوا بِهَا عَنْ كُلِّ مَا سِوَاهَا، فَإِذَا قَرَأَهُ بِتَفَكُّرٍ حَتَّى إِذَا مَرَّ بِآيَةٍ هُوَ مُحْتَاجٌ إِلَيْهَا فِي شِفَاءِ قَلْبِهِ كَرَّرَهَا وَلَوْ مِائَةَ مَرَّةٍ، وَلَوْ لَيْلَةً كَامِلَةً.

"If one knows the reward of reciting the Qur'ān meditatively, they will busy themselves with it alone. If one comes across an ayah he really needs to heal his heart; he should repeat it even a hundred times or even for as long as a full night."

Reciting the Qur'ān meditatively is the main reason for setting heart right. Ibn Mas'ūd (رضي الله عنه) said,

لَا تَهُذُّوا الْقُرْآنَ هَذَّ الشِّعْرِ، وَلَا تَنْثُرُوهُ نَثْرَ الدَّقْلِ، وَقِفُوا عِنْدَ عَجَائِبِهِ وَحَرِّكُوا بِهِ الْقُلُوبَ، وَلَا يَكُنْ هَمُّ أَحَدِكُمْ آخِرَ السُّورَةِ.

"Do not recite the Qur'ān like poetry, and do not spit it out like you do with bad dates. Reflect on its wonders, and make it move your hearts. Do not be interested only in reaching the end of the Sūrah."[17]

Whoever sought to mend and called for it should stick to the Qur'ān and the Sunnah.

This Ummah cannot be reformed by sects, groups or innovated ideas. The only way to reform the Ummah is to stick to the Qur'ān and the Sunnah with the understanding of the Salaf. Whoever took this way will be a reformer. However, whoever left it, and preferred to take another way hoping to find a way out of the tribulations, or joined a group or a party, apart from the Qur'ān and the Sunnah. Such

---

[17] Related by al-Bayhaqī in *Shu'ab al-'Imān* 1/344, Sunan Abū Dāwud 2/77. One came to Ibn Mas'ūd and said, "I recite Al-Mufassil (long sura) in one Rak'ah." Ibn Mas'ūd replied, **"You recite Qur'ān like poetry and spit it out like bad dates?"** Abū Sulaymān Al-Khaṭṭābī commented, **"He refers to the fast recitation. He blamed him for that because fast recitation causes one not to understand the Qur'ān or realize its meanings."** Ma'lim As-Sunan 1/283

way of thinking will definitely make its follower a corruptor and will sink him into trials, and will end up leading the Ummah to a great evil.

STARTING WITH OURSELVES

If we want to reform ourselves and others, we must start with ourselves. We should keep ourselves as close as possible to the Qur'ān and the Sunnah with the best understanding of the companions of the Prophet (ﷺ).

We should convey this message to our wives, sons and daughters, and teach them to memorize the Qur'ān, to recite meditatively, and to practice the teachings of the Qur'ān following the steps of the Salaf (رضي الله عنه). So, if we build our families and communities upon this *Manhaj* (way of life) we will live in well-being and happiness.

I beseech Allāh, with His Most Beautiful Names and Attributes to grant us good hearts and set right our hearts by His words, and to make our hearts fear and unify Him, and to make us a mean for bringing every goodness and preventing every evil, and to make us a mercy for the believers, and mercy for the countries and servants.

Moreover, Allāh knows best, and Prayers and blessings be upon our Prophet (ﷺ).